•BODY BITS•

EYE-POPPING PLANT PART FACTS

by Paul Mason and Dave Smith

Gareth Stevens
CLASSROOM

Please visit our website, www.garethstevens.com. For a free color catalog of all our high-quality books, call toll free 1-800-542-2595 or fax 1-877-542-2596.

Cataloging-in-Publication Data
Names: Mason, Paul. | Smith, Dave.
Title: Eye-popping plant part facts / by Paul Mason and Dave Smith.
Description: New York : Gareth Stevens Publishing, 2023. | Series: Body bits | Includes glossary and index.
Identifiers: ISBN 9781538277775 (pbk.) | ISBN 9781538277799 (library bound) | ISBN 9781538277782 (6pack) | ISBN 9781538277805 (ebook)
Subjects: LCSH: Plant physiology--Juvenile literature. | Plants--Juvenile literature.
Classification: LCC QK711.5 M37 2023 | DDC 581--dc23

Published in 2023 by
Gareth Stevens Publishing
29 E. 21st Street
New York, NY 10010

Editors: Melanie Palmer and Grace Glendinning
Designer: Peter Scoulding
Illustrations: Dave Smith

Picture Credits
Alamy: Blickwinkel 23l; Malagasy View 9b; Mike Read 25bl. Dreamstime: Whiskeybottle 11c. Nature PL: Nick Upton 22. Science Photo Library: Merlin D Tuttle 13. Shutterstock: Sergei Aleshin 20r; Paul Aniszewski 7; Archaeopteryx Tours 21b; Atiger 25br; Darryl Brooks 14b; Dan Campbell 21c; Ms Jane Campbell 14t; Jason Champaigne 17; Chrispo 19c; Alessandro Colle 19l; Nita Corfe 5b; Cotosa 10; Cpaulfell 16b; CTatiana 28; Damann 4; Judy M Darby 16c; Anthony Fergus 18l; Guentermanaus 24r; Ahmad Haroun 23b; Jens Heidler 20l; Cathy Keifer 20c; Le Do 29tr; Ingrid Maasik 27r; Alyshia MacD 12b; Paul Marcus 25t; Medhals 5t; Ruud Morijn 15; Yakov Oskanov 9t; Anne Powell 11b; Rapin_1981 23r; Jane Rix 29b; Olga Rybnikova 19r; Arda Savasciogullari 24l; Somsak2503; Geoff Sperring 8; Linas T 18r; Unique Vision 21t; Viktorishy 26; Mrs Ya 25cr; Yakonstant 11t; Zerbor 29tl; Alessandro Zocc 18c.

Printed in the United States of America

CPSIA compliance information: Batch #CSGS23: For further information contact Gareth Stevens, New York, New York at 1-800-542-2595.

Find us on

Contents

The weird world of plant parts

Plants live on land, in the rivers and seas, and even up in the air in trees*. They are staggeringly good at adapting to different environments.

*Air plants (from a genus called *Tillandsia*) don't need soil. Instead, their leaves absorb moisture from the air.

Plants and places

From high mountains to dry deserts, wet-and-warm rainforests to freezing plains, plants find ways to survive. To do this, they have evolved all kinds of weird - sometimes eye-popping - parts.

Very sharp!

Up to 15 cm long

NO GIANT SLOTHS — OR — SHORT-FACED BEARS

The honey locust tree has bark dotted with spikes that developed thousands of years ago to keep away giant sloths and short-faced bears. These animals no longer exist - but the spikes are still there.

These parts might be giant thorn clusters or poison-filled leaves to keep animals from having them for dinner. They might be specially scented flowers or complicated leaf shapes that attract animals. Some plants want help with reproduction, and some want something else an animal can provide ... such as poo.

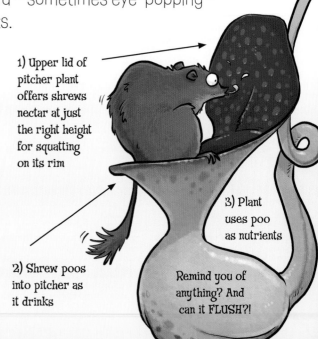

1) Upper lid of pitcher plant offers shrews nectar at just the right height for squatting on its rim

2) Shrew poos into pitcher as it drinks

3) Plant uses poo as nutrients

Remind you of anything? And can it FLUSH?!

Clever plants

Not all plants are quite what they seem – some have sticky pads or traps that catch insects or even bigger animals ... which the plant then eats!

Watch out, flies – carnivorous Venus flytrap about!

SCIENCE FLASH

For most plants, life starts from a seed. The seed begins a cycle that allows plants to reproduce and spread.

Inside the seed is a tiny plant with its own food supply.

Most seeds need water, soil, and sunlight to start growing.

The stem grows to the light, while roots grow down into the soil.

Once its leaves unfold, the plant can use photosynthesis to make food for itself.

When big enough, many plants make flowers containing pollen, then seeds. The whole process begins again.

Ancient plants

There are plant species that have survived on Earth since the time of the dinosaurs.

RAWR

Tyrannosaurus rex: lived 68–65 million years ago.

Wollemi pine*: lived 200 million years ago and still lives.

*Not actually a pine tree

Roots have ears

A plant's roots draw in water, without which it will die. This makes finding water a key job. Some plants have an amazing way of doing this.

Good listeners

You might not think that plants can hear, but scientists in Australia recently discovered that some plants find moisture using sound. Their roots grow toward the sound of water.

If the idea of plants being able to hear is jaw-dropping, how about these extra facts:

- the plants could also tell when the sound was a recording of water, rather than the real thing

- they could even tell whether it was water from a natural source (which they liked and grew toward) or from a tap (which they didn't).

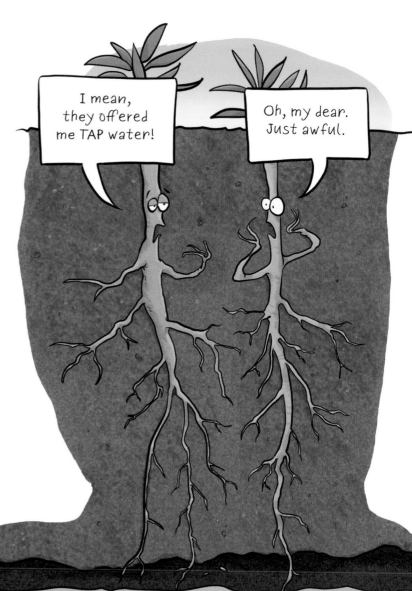

SCIENCE FLASH

How do plants drink? Scientists investigating the giant sequoia tree found that the process for these towering trees, called transpiration, is powered by water evaporation from the leaves. As water is released from the leaves, it creates a sucking effect. The whole tree becomes a giant straw, and water is pulled into the roots.

Tree-root telegraph

Plants can not only listen, they can also talk – to each other, at least. The tips of tree roots connect with a network of fungi that spreads through the woodlands. Some trees, such as beech trees, use this network to communicate. They pass messages from tree to tree using chemicals, hormones, and even slow electrical pulses.

Some trees also use the fungal network to share resources. They send water and sugar to saplings, for example, helping them to survive long enough to grow to the light. Beech trees also use the network to keep alive the stumps of their cut-down relatives – sometimes for centuries.

RIP CHARLES

What did Charles ever do to them?

We've been neighbors for years.

Surprising seeds

Seeds are the secret of plants' success. Seeds are the parts of plants that allow a species to spread and, sometimes, to survive in incredibly hostile environments.

How come WE can't have roots, Mom?

But I want roots NOW!

You can grow roots when the next rain comes!

Waiting game

In deserts and other inhospitable places, plant seeds can lie dormant for years. In Australia, for example, a Sturt's desert pea seed waits in the soil until rains come. In just a few days it puts down deep roots, grows, and flowers. Then its seeds spread out and lie in the ground until the next rains – which may not come for many years.

Blown on the wind

Most of us have seen "helicopters," the seeds of sycamore and maple trees, spinning through the air. In South Africa, the candelabra lily has a different way of using the wind to spread its seeds.

1) It grows a bright, colorful flowering head like a candelabra. When the time comes, this dries out and falls away from the plant.

2) The dried-out candelabra cartwheels along in the wind, throwing out seeds as it goes.

Ping!　Plop!　Tonk!　Boing!

WHEEEE!

The world's biggest seed

The plant world's biggest seed comes from the coco de mer palm tree, which grows on just two islands in the Indian Ocean. Experts think that its seeds are so big because the seedlings have to grow in the shadow of their parents. The huge seeds provide them with extra nutrients until they get big enough to reach the light.

Seeds weighing 40 pounds (18 kg)

98 feest (30 m) above ground

Unsuspecting tourist

Special seeds for lemurs

In Madagascar, the traveler's palm has special seeds that attract the island's lemurs. The lemurs can only see green and blue – so the tree has bright blue seeds. The tree is not really a palm. It is related to bird-of-paradise plants. It's probably called a "traveler" because the base of each leaf collects almost a quart (1 l) of water, helpful for a thirsty traveler.

That IS impressive.

YUCK!

Once they have eaten the blue traveler's palm seeds, the lemurs move on to a new location. They poo the seeds out again – which is a bit disgusting, but does help the plant spread.

Plants in disguise

Not all plants actually look like plants. Instead, some grow into shapes that disguise them as something completely different.

Monkey face orchids

Monkey face orchids grow in Central and South America. They got their name because they look like a monkey's face – but this is just an accident. The shape's real purpose is to look like local mushrooms. The orchid also smells like these mushrooms, so it attracts lots of mushroom-loving fungus gnats. As they crawl over the plant looking for non-existent mushrooms, the gnats are tricked into collecting and delivering pollen.

Not much of a talker, are you?

It's not hard to see how the monkey face orchid got its name.

Rare orchid

High on the slopes of Mount Kinabalu in Borneo, just a few Rothschild's slipper orchids grow. Parts of the plant are covered in clusters of little dots. These dots look like tiny bugs called aphids – but they are not. So why does the plant have these parts?

Female wasps like to lay eggs among the "aphids," so that the young wasps will have something to eat when they hatch.

The wasp becomes trapped – the only way out is an escape hatch at the bottom of the plant.

While inside, the wasp collects orchid pollen on her body, which she then carries to the next plant.

Bee orchids not only look like female bees, but also give off a scent that SMELLS like female bees. By the time a love-struck male bee realizes, it has been covered in pollen.

To a male sawfly, the flowers of a flying duck orchid look like a female sawfly. As they try to mate with the "female," the male flies have a dusting of pollen stuck to their backs.

Pitfalls and other traps

Pitfall traps are found on pitcher plants. Their leaves grow into a large, bowl-like shape filled with digestive juices. Animals can fall into these traps and drown.

The pitcher of no escape

In Borneo, little rodents sometimes try to drink the nectar of king pitcher plants – and it turns out to be the last drink they ever have. This pitcher is so big that it can hold several quarts of liquid. Its nectar-coated cap sits at an angle just right for tree shrews to sit and lick (and poo), but is a bit too wide open for smaller animals. A little creature that slips in cannot escape, and drowns. The plant is pleased – it gets extra nutrients.

Aaaah!

Whooaaa, man ...

SLIP!

The slide of death

The trumpet pitcher has a slippery surface, which causes insects to slip and slide off the rim and into its digestive juices. Experts have recently found that the plant also releases a relaxing smell that makes insects wobbly on their feet. At least the insects die feeling chilled out.

The bat hotel

Also in the mountains of Borneo, the bat pitcher plant gets nutrients from bat poo, not drowned bats. The plant has a special ridge inside its pitcher, which is a comfortable resting place for little woolly bats. Not only that, the plant's shape is particularly good at reflecting bat sonar, making the bat pitcher easy for them to find. The bat hangs out there all day, dropping plenty of poo into the pitcher, before it flies off for a night's hunting.

Sigh ... never any privacy.

The tunnel of terror

The parrot pitcher has a very cunning technique for catching prey. It uses a combination of scent and a clever shape to draw insects to their death.

Oooh! Yum!

A delicious smell tempts insects to go through a tiny entrance.

Once inside, they look for a way out. Bright white spots on the pitcher's walls look like exits - but aren't. The insect follows the spots further into the plant.

At the end of the narrow passage are downward-pointing hairs, which stop the insect from turning back. It eventually becomes so tired from trying that it falls into the plant's digestive juices.

Fish catcher

When the swamps (where the parrot pitchers live) flood, it even catches small fish in its deadly trap!

13

Poison producers

Plants have evolved many ways of protecting themselves. One of these is to be poisonous to anything that eats – or even touches – them.

The world's most dangerous tree?

Manchineel trees grow on lands in and around the Caribbean Sea. They are sometimes called "beach apple" trees, which sounds quite nice. One of manchineel's other names, though, gives you a better clue of what this plant is like. In Spanish, it is called *arbol de la muerte* – "tree of death." Manchineels have a LOT of poisonous parts, but the two worst are its sap and its fruit.

A manchineel is not a good tree to shelter under when it's raining. The rainwater washes dangerous sap down on to you.

Sap: poisonous

Touching manchineel sap burns your skin, which blisters and goes red. It is extremely painful. The sap can cause headaches, make it hard to breathe, and even lead to temporary blindness.

Fruit: poisonous

Manchineel apples taste sweet, but don't be tempted. They cause stomach pain, difficulty swallowing, vomiting, internal bleeding, and damage to your digestive system. They may even cause death.

Manchineel trees are so dangerous that people place "Do not touch" signs on them as a warning.

SCIENCE FLASH

Sap is a fluid inside plants. Its job is to carry water, nutrients, and other chemicals around the plant. It has a similar job to blood in humans and other animals.

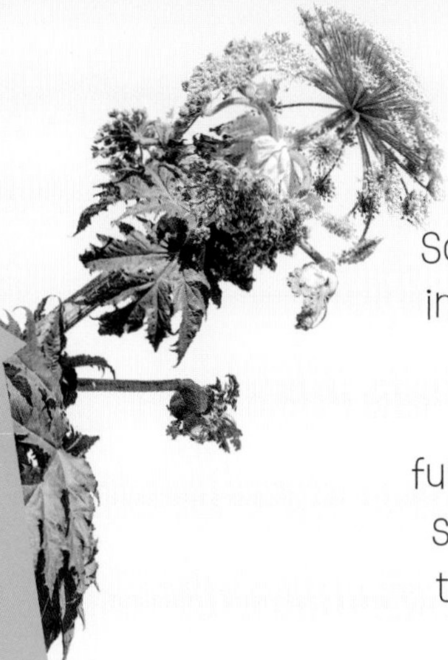

Horrid hogweed

Some kinds of hogweed that live in Europe and North America are definitely best avoided. Their sap contains chemicals called furocoumarins. When exposed to sunlight, these chemicals cause terrible blisters. Getting the sap in your eyes could even cause blindness.

The pain bush

If you ever visit southern Africa, watch out for the pain bush. (The clue about why is in its name.) The sap of this plant causes human skin to blister and become highly painful. Its effects last a few days, sometimes longer.

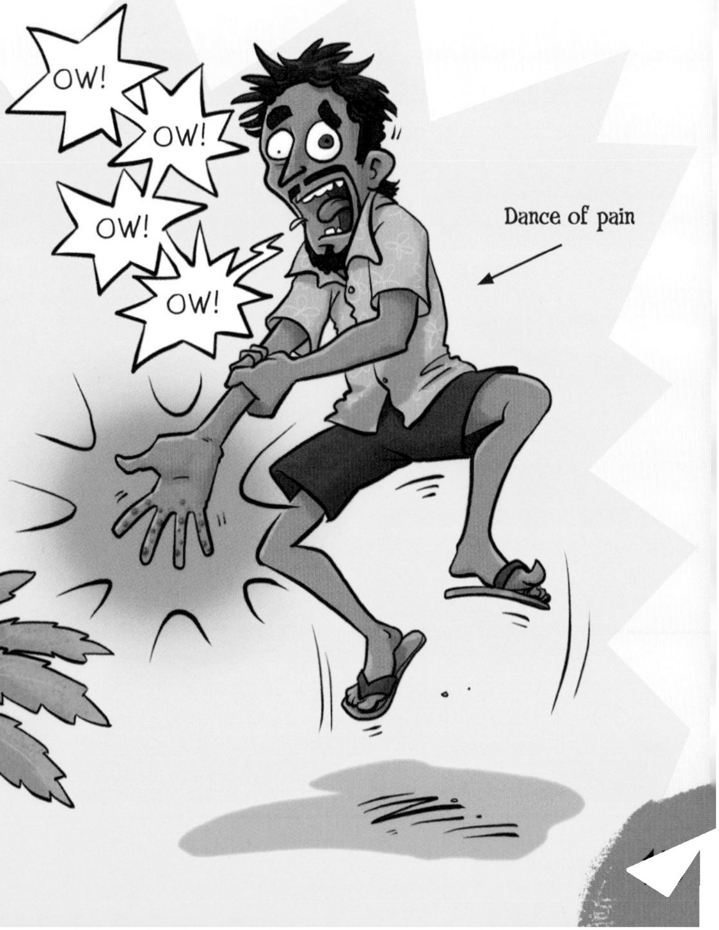

OW!
OW!
OW!
OW!
Dance of pain

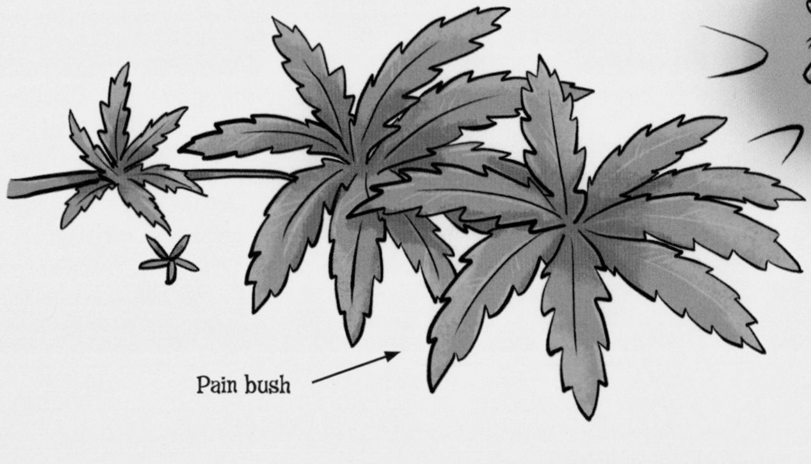

Pain bush

Spines and thorns

Many plants grow spines or thorns. These are useful in lots of ways, but are particularly good at putting off hungry creatures.

SCIENCE FLASH

Spines and thorns are different things. A spine is a kind of adapted leaf and grows from the same spot as a leaf. Thorns grow from the same part of the plant as branches, and are technically adapted stems or branches.

Tough climb.

Very uncomfortable.

The spines on horse nettle plants are there to stop passing animals eating them. They also make it harder for insects to climb up to the leaves for a nibble.

Spiky protection

Acacia trees have developed a neat spiny trick. If goats (which have very tough mouths) eat the acacia, it starts to grow longer spines at goat-mouth height to stop them.

I'm sure this was less spiny last time.

Ow!

The unclimbable tree?

If there's one tree you really would NOT want to climb, it's the honey locust. The tree has thorns everywhere. Usually they grow in massive clumps that look a bit like something a ninja might throw at you. The biggest thorns can reach 6 inches (15 cm) long and are extremely tough. In the past, honey locust thorns are said to have been used as nails.

Cactus spines

There are nearly 2,000 different species of cactus and all of them grow spines.* Usually these spines are to protect the plant from animals trying to eat it or get at the water stored inside. But cactus spines have other jobs too.

*A few cactus species only have spines when young.

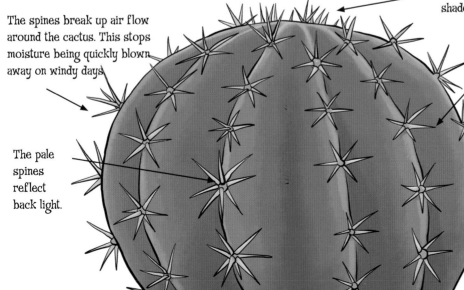

Lots of thin spines together can shade a cactus from sun damage.

The spines break up air flow around the cactus. This stops moisture being quickly blown away on windy days.

On foggy or misty days, or early in the morning, moisture collects on the spines. Drops gather and run down the cactus to its roots.

The pale spines reflect back light.

The barrel cactus is so well adapted to desert life that it can live for over 100 years.

Snap! And you're lunch

A few plants can do something we don't normally think plants can manage: move with lightning speed. What's more, they use this speed to trap - and then eat - animals.

I'm outta here.

Feed me!

The most famous fast-moving plant is the Venus flytrap. It is unusual in lots of ways, with several eye-popping parts that help it trap prey. Speed is not its only trick, though - the Venus flytrap can also count.

Mmm ...

1) The leaves produce sweet nectar in their nectar glands. Passing flies smell a tempting meal.

Nectar glands

2) Inside each leaf are teeny-tiny hairs. If a fly touches a hair, the flytrap's timer starts running. The fly now has 20 seconds to live or die. The plant waits for another hair to be touched, to be sure it's really a fly wandering about.

3) If the fly touches a hair for a second time, the flytrap's leaves snap shut. This movement can take as little as 0.1 of a second. It has to be fast, as you will know if you've ever tried to swat a fly.

SCIENCE FLASH

How does a Venus flytrap snap shut? Scientists have discovered that an electrical signal starts the process. It causes the leaves to change rapidly from a curved-in shape to a curved-out one. This double 'popping' movement is what closes the trap. Exactly how this movement happens is still not known.

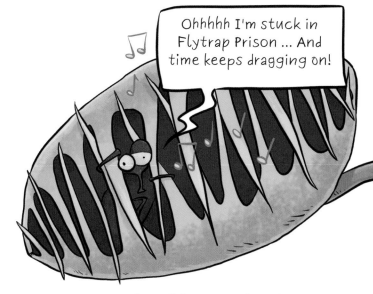

Ohhhhh I'm stuck in Flytrap Prison ... And time keeps dragging on!

Ferdinand! He's a shell of his former self!

Venus flytraps are so fascinating that people like to keep them as pot plants. Unfortunately, most plants were originally collected from the wild, where they are becoming increasingly rare.

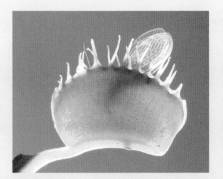

4) The flytrap's leaf edges lock together, forming prison bars to trap the fly. As it struggles to break free, the fly touches more hairs. The leaves squeeze tighter and the plant releases digestive juice to remove nutrients from the fly's body.

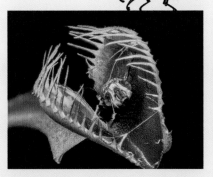

5) Days later, the trap reopens. Inside is the empty body shell of the fly, which will blow away on the wind.

6) The plant prepares for its next meal – unless it has now snapped shut four or five times. Each trap can only snap shut a few times before it dies and falls off the plant.

In any garden or park, you'll probably find lots of plants with leaves and stems that are covered in tiny hairs.
But what do plants need hairs for?

Sticky sundews

There are lots of species of sundew, ranging from thumb-sized plants to plants as tall as an eight-year-old. But they all have a very special part: hairs on their surface that produce a sticky liquid. On every continent except Antarctica, sundew plants live in bogs and marshes. These places often lack soil nutrients, so the sundews have found ways to supplement their diet – with meat.

Ooey, gooey goodness!

No, wait, what?

HELP!

Suddenly not hungry ...

I AM!

1) If you're an insect, the sundew's liquid smells almost irresistible.

2) When the insect lands on the sundew, it realizes it has made a terrible mistake. Sticky hairs curl inward and close around the insect.

3) The fly becomes exhausted and coated in the sticky fluid. It struggles to escape, but cannot. Eventually it dies. The plant's digestive juices get to work on extracting nutrients.

Stinging hairs

Many of us have accidentally brushed against a stinging plant, then wished we'd been more careful as a painful rash springs up. In the stinging nettle plant, the pain comes from tiny hairs on the nettle's leaves, which are tipped with a mixture of at least three pain-and-itch-producing chemicals. The sting is not very nice, but usually disappears within a short time. Other plants, though, have evolved more-dangerous hairs ...

The stinging bush

In northern Australia, watch out for the stinging bush (also called gympie-gympie). Its tiny hairs can get embedded in your skin, where they release a neurotoxin, a poison that affects the nervous system. The effects can last for months in humans. If the area is touched, gets wet, heats up or cools down, it starts to sting again.

Don't ...

come ...

any ...

closer!

Tread-softly

Tread-softly is also called finger-rot and noseburn. You would know why if you ever touched it, then picked your nose. Like the stinging bush, its hairs break off and release a stinging, irritating chemical. Unlike the stinging bush, the pain "only" lasts a few days in worst-case situations.

Jailhouse plants

Some plants have parts that allow them to imprison insects – but not so that they can eat them. These plants just want to put the insects in jail until they help with pollination.

Arum flowers: not for sniffing

The *arum maculatum*, also known as the "cuckoo pint" plant, uses tiny flies to help it pollinate. First, the arum grows a little rod of tiny flowers, called a spadix. These flowers smell of pee and poo and general decay. Flies LOVE this smell, so they soon arrive in swarms.

The spadix is even warm like fresh poo and rotting meat – but any flies that crawl to where the smell is strongest soon realize their mistake. Downward-pointing hairs trap the little insects overnight. While they are in jail, they are showered with pollen. In the morning, the hairs collapse, and the flies (which never learn their lesson) are released to pollinate another arum.

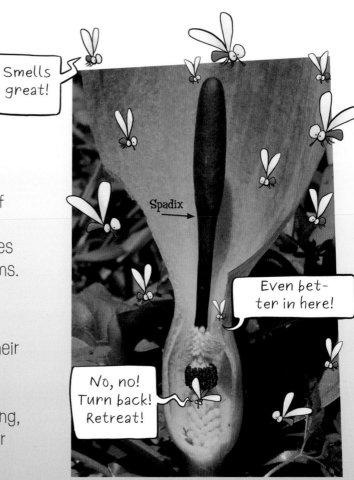

Dutchman's pipes

A Dutchman's pipe is not the kind of pipe a Dutchman (or woman) could smoke; it is a kind of plant. It uses smells, tricks, traps, and downward-facing hairs to hold insects prisoner.

Keep your mouth OFF the flower.

Aristolochia arborea is a species of Dutchman's pipe that grows in Central America. It grows at the base of trees, where mushrooms also grow. At the heart of its flower is an imitation mushroom and the plant also gives off a mushroom smell.

Fungus gnats can't resist the smell, and get temporarily trapped by the flower's jailhouse hairs. These mother gnats are looking for a place to lay their eggs, but they are also collecting and delivering pollen in the process. Unfortunately, when the eggs hatch, they soon discover there's nothing for them to eat and they die.

But it smells so goooooood …

These two should not be mixed up.

Who knew? BOTH kinds of pipe are linked to cancer. Don't smoke, kids!

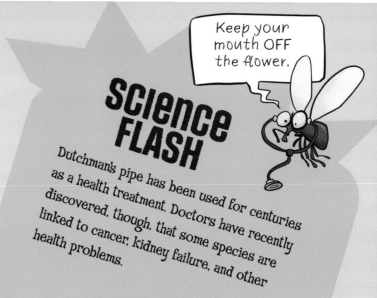

23

The world's stinkiest plants

Many plants smell sweet – but not all. You've just read about pee, poo, and mushroom smells ... but it gets worse. Here are some rivals for the title of World's Stinkiest Plant.

The smell of death

Some insects love to lay their eggs in the rotting flesh of dead animals, also known as carrion. This is because the dead meat gives their young something to eat as they grow. Cleverly, some plants use the smell of death to attract insects. Believe it or not, the four flowers you see here all smell like death ... on purpose!

Starfish flower

This plant uses death-scent to attract carrion flies to lay eggs on the surface of its flowers. As the flies crawl about, they collect and leave behind pollen. The flower's trick goes even further – it grows soft, white hairs all over so it also feels like animal fur.

Corpse flowers

These smell so terrible, it's a good thing that each plant only flowers every few years. The rest of the time, the plant stores up energy in an underground structure called a corm. By the time it flowers, the corm can weigh as much as a grown man. The flower grows rapidly and only lasts for about 36 hours before it dies. By then, though, thousands of insects have helped pollinate the plant.

YUCK!

Durian fruit smells so bad, it is banned from public transport in Singapore. Its smell has been compared to old gym socks, a skunk, onions, garlic, and stinky cheese. Amazingly, its fruit is actually very tasty and is a popular food in Asia, where the durian grows.

No durians

Dead-horse arum

This plant achieves pollination in a similar way to cuckoo pint, which you read about on page 22, but it smells even worse. In fact, many people say the smell of rotting animal is so bad that this is the world's stinkiest plant.

Extreme survivors

Plants live in all kinds of places, from high mountains to dry deserts. But which plants are the most extreme, and what amazing parts help them to survive?

Mangroves

Most plants cannot drink salty water. The mangrove tree, though, has eye-popping tricks that allow it to live beside the sea.

4) Some trees send the remaining salt to old leaves or bark, which fall off.

3) Some trees push salt out through specialized leaves (which taste salty when licked) and store fresh water in thick, wax-coated leaves.

2) Roots in the air "breathe" in oxygen through tiny pores, which close up under water.

1) Mangrove roots filter out up to 90 percent of the salt. (What's left would still kill most plants.)

Tumbleweed

Tumbleweed is a desert plant. When conditions become too dry, tumbleweeds separate from their roots. The wind rolls them away. When the plant reaches a place with more water, it swells up and releases seeds. New tumbleweeds start to grow in their new home.

Mountain survivors

Life up a mountain is tough for plants. In summer, the sun is powerful enough to burn you, but it is freezing at night.

To keep their buds warm, snow willows use color. The plant's buds are black, which absorbs the sun's heat. They are also covered by a layer of tiny white hairs, which trap heat and keep it warm through the night.

Purple saxifrage grows in the high mountains (and the Arctic). Its leaves are tiny and thick, and they overlap like fish scales to keep in warmth.

Even more eye-popping, purple saxifrage is sometimes able to form a chalky shield against the wind, which is made of the same material clams use to make their shells.

Purple saxifrage grows slowly, but it is very determined.

8-inch (20 cm) wide plant = 20–40 years old

Do you speak plant?

Scientists have recently begun to understand that plants send messages to each other far more than we previously thought possible. They do this mostly through the use of chemicals.

You called?

Grass

The smell of cut grass is often listed among the smells people love - but this smell is actually a distress signal. It developed as a warning against insect attack.

The smell has two purposes. First, it warns other grasses that an attack may be coming and they should prepare anti-insect chemical defenses. The smell also summons nearby wasps to come and attack the grass-eating insects.

Ahh! Watch out! *Battle stations!* *Send out the smells!*

Like grass, broad beans release chemicals to warn their neighbors that an attack is coming. The neighbors repay them by releasing chemicals that repel insects and call in attack wasps.

Watch out, Brenda.

Poplar and sugar maple trees send each other warnings when they are attacked.

Got it. Chemical weapons deployed.

Acacia trees

Acacia trees grow a lot of long spines to stop animals eating them. Giraffes, though, have long, leaf-plucking tongues, thick lips, and hard palates. They are not put off by the spines – so acacias have another defense ...

1) Giraffe starts to eat acacia tree's leaves

2) Acacia releases a chemical called tannin into its leaves

3) Tree sends out a cloud of ethylene gas

Yuk!

4) Nearby acacias sense the gas and release tannin into their leaves too

5) Giraffe looks for something else to eat

Happy plants?

As far as scientists can tell today, plants mostly use their networks to send warnings and other important signals – but maybe we just haven't yet figured out what plants talk about when they're happy.

I don't like acacia that much anyway...

29

Glossary

Arctic cold region in the far northern parts of Earth, close to the North Pole; Arctic lands are frozen for much of the year and very cold in winter

bark tough outer covering of the trunk and branches of a tree or other plant

body shell hard outer layer of an animal, such as an insect; another name for a body shell is exoskeleton

bud small, tightly formed part of a plant that grows into a flower or leaf

candelabra large holder with many branches that fit lightbulbs or candles

carrion rotting flesh of a dead animal

distress great worry, pain, or fear

dormant in a sleep-like state, but with normal functions, such as breathing, digestion, and growth, either slowed down or stopped

evaporation changing from liquid to vapor (vapor is tiny particles of liquid that have spread into the air)

evolve develop special characteristics over a long period of time (individual animals do not evolve, but species do)

filter screen out or remove

fungus non-plants, such as mushrooms, toadstools, mold, and yeast that reproduce by sending out little units called spores

genus group of animals or plants that are very similar to each other and closely related. In the classification of living things, genus comes above species. Animals in the same species are able to reproduce; animals from the same genus but different species cannot reproduce.

gnat small fly that looks a bit like a very little mosquito and usually appears in large swarms

high tide time during the day when the level of the sea is at its highest

hormone chemical that carries messages within living things, telling them how to act; for example, hormones can tell your heart to beat faster, or tell your body to grow (or stop growing)

mate produce young

m.y.a. short for: million years ago

nectar sweet, energy-rich fluid

neurotoxin a poison that affects the nervous system

ninja Japanese martial arts expert famous for skill at unarmed combat and using unusual weapons

nutrient something that a living thing needs to grow and/or survive

palate roof or top part of a mouth

photosynthesis process used by green plants to obtain nutrients from the gas carbon dioxide and water; to do this the plants also need sunlight

pollen powdery substance released by the male part of a plant; when spread to the female part of a plant from the same species, pollen causes the plant to reproduce

rare very unusual

rash raised, red, itchy area of skin

reproduce produce offspring (for example, when a cat has kittens or a tree produces a seedling)

sap fluid inside plants that carries water, nutrients, and other chemicals where they are needed

seedling young plant grown from a seed

Finding out more

Books to read

From plants that disguise themselves as pebbles (to avoid the attention of hungry tortoises), to a cactus that lives on bird poo, find out about some more fascinating plants in:

Perfectly Peculiar Plants by Chris Thorogood and Catell Ronca (words & pictures, 2018). Chris is also the author of *Weird Plants* (Kew Publishing, 2018), which is for adults but would be interesting for a confident reader.

If you're looking for basic facts about plants in a simple, easy-to-read format, head for the library and grab a copy of one or more from:
Amazing Science: Plants by Sally Hewitt (Wayland, 2014)
Roots, Stems, Leaves and Flowers by Ruth Owen (Ruby Tuesday Books, 2016)
All About Plants by Peter Riley (Franklin Watts, 2016)

Finally, if all this reading about plants has made you want to go and grow some, a great way to start would be to get your hands on a copy of one of these:

Gardening Projects for Kids: Fantastic Ideas for Making Things, Growing Plants and Flowers and *Attracting Wildlife* by Jenny Hendy (Southwater, 2011)
Let's Get Gardening Royal Horticultural Society (DK Children, 2019)
The Kew Gardens Children's Cookbook: Plant, Cook, Eat by Caroline Craig (Wayland, 2016)

Index